The Woman in the Text

A collection of essays addressing controversial topics about women in Islam: from 'wife-beating' and divorce, to inheritance and 'A'isha's union to the Prophet

In the name of God, the Most Wise, the Most Just

.

To my dear family

*Especially **all** of my beloved children*

If it wasn't for them, this would have been completed much, much earlier

Contents Page

Introduction

This booklet is a collection of various essays that deal with several pressing issues surrounding the various legal and judicial rulings concerning women in Islam. These issues have been popularised – fallaciously and inaccurately, for the most part – by both the Western media and Orientalist detractors.

Perhaps one of the most pivotal and important topics addressed is the age of 'Aisha at which she completed her divine union with the Prophet Muhammad (PBUH). I attempt to display and dissect the philosophical underpinnings of the morality framework utilised by critiques of this union, notwithstanding the historical and sometimes anachronistic reasoning used by examining the age of sexual consent in different societies across different time periods. Most importantly, I address the inbuilt mechanism of the *Shari'ah* due to the principles of Islamic jurisprudence (*Usūl al-Fiqh*) in protecting and safeguarding any future spouse from harm, irrespective of the age of consent.

In a separate paper, the infamous thirty-fourth verse from the fourth chapter the Qur'an (4:34) is addressed. Several important themes that run throughout the verse are discussed, including the supposed endorsement of 'wife-beating' and the viewpoints held therein by both traditional exegetes and jurists as well as modern interpretations. The primary focus of the latter interpretations is Amina Wadud and her unique hermeneutical position of 'just say no'. I also explore the concept of a supposed patriarchal form of obedience to a male disciplinary figure. Likewise, the concept and interpretation of *qiwāmah* is discussed. I explore the different translations of the term that encompass the support placed on males on their spouses, to female witness testimony, and the complexities and differences between *ishhad* (being summoned voluntarily to witness a monetary transaction) and legal testimony in a court of law. An offshoot of this discussion included an exploration of female *hadith* narration (*riwāyah*) throughout the ages.

The final two short essays in this book discuss the questions of whether Islam subjugates married women in an inescapable relationship, and whether the intricate rulings of Islamic inheritance unjustly favour men over women.

I would like to thank all those who assisted and advised during the writing of these essays. Their contributions have been dear and invaluable.

Abu Safiyyah Mohammed Osman

29/04/19

London, UK.

On Morality: The Union Of The Prophet (PBUH) With *Ā'isha*

Introduction

The question of the union of Prophet Muhammad (peace be upon him) to *'Ā'isha* at a young age requires a preliminary philosophical analysis of morality. It is from this particular lens that popular detractors uphold a narrative in which the Prophet Muhammad (PBUH) was uniquely depraved in his insistence on marrying and consummating *'Ā'isha* (his third wife) at the age of 9. This essay is an attempt to expose the fallacious reasoning employed by such popular detractors and to demonstrate the philosophical double standards of the proponents of their views. In the first part of this essay, we will investigate the philosophical frameworks utilised and evaluate their use as ultimate barometers of truth. Secondly, we will evaluate how orientalist detractors judge the sexual age of consent in any given society and analyse whether or not such commentators are fallaciously anachronistic in their historical reasoning. Moreover, a comparative analysis will be made between Islam and other religions with respect to sexual age for consent. The concept of adolescence in determining adulthood will also be briefly examined, together with the role of principles of Islamic jurisprudence *(Usūl al-Fiqh)* in the issue of harm and its relevance to the validity of marriage and the age of consent. Lastly, we will consider the recorded statements of *'Ā'isha* herself in relation to this union. To be clear, what is not advocated in this essay is a legal reconsideration of the age of consent in the UK or any other country in the world. Rather, this essay aims to question the fallacious reasoning used by detractors insistent on questioning the morality of this divinely sanctioned union.

Margoliouth's Observation

One of earliest known sources containing criticism against the marriage of Prophet Muhammad (PBUH) to *'Ā'isha* is *Mohammad and the Rise of Islam*, written by the British Orientalist David Margoliouth (d. 1940) and published in 1905. Margoliouth labels the marriage an 'ill-assorted union ... for as such we must characterise the marriage of a man of fifty-three to a child of nine'.[1] It is significant to note that the union of the Prophet (PBUH) to *'Ā'isha* was one that was categorically accepted in 7th Century Arabia - a claim that could be extended to many other parts of the world, as we will shortly observe. Virtually no criticism of this union can be found even from the most ardent detractors of the time, such as the Prophet's (PBUH) paternal uncle and fervent disparager of Islam, *Abu Lahab*, who was also the namesake of a scathing chapter in the *Qur'ān*.

Furthermore, *Ibn Sa'd* (d. 230 AH) narrates in his *al-Tabaqāt* that *'Ā'isha* was previously engaged to one of the nobles of the *Quraysh* prior to her engagement with Prophet Muhammad (PBUH).[2] Extending this line of reasoning, we can note that even in the following generations after the passing of the Prophet Muhammad (PBUH), there are no known historical sources that make mention of this union in a negative light, neither from adherents of other religions nor from self-proclaimed Islamic reformists. Even from the earliest Orientalist accounts, criticism was not generally directed at this issue. For example, the main studies in the 18th Century conducted on Islam and Muslims were silent on this issue being one of depravity and immorality. Examples include Simon Ockley (d. 1720) in *History of the Saracens*,[3] Humphrey Prideaux (d. 1724) in *The True Nature of Imposture*,[4] and Edward Gibbon (d. 1794) in *The History of the Decline and Fall of the Roman Empire.*[5] Ironically, Prideaux justifies the age in which the marriage was consummated using a psychological reasoning that he extends to other countries and climates. Moreover, studies conducted in the 19th Century contain no criticism against this issue. These works include *Muslim Studies*[6] by Ignác Goldziher (d. 1921), *The Genuine Islam*[7] by George Bernard Shaw (d. 1950), and *On Heroes, Hero-worship, and the Heroic in History*[8] by Thomas Carlyle (d. 1881). These examples demonstrate that the argument against this specific marriage is relatively new, one not previously coined by even the most ardent detractors to the Prophet (PBUH), from his time until the beginning of the 20th Century.

A Distinct Progression

Criticism of the marriage between the Prophet (PBUH) and *'Ā'isha* has since matured into the denunciation that the Prophet (PBUH) was a paedophile. This accusation is used particularly by far-right

11

groups and the most fervent critics of Islam. Paedophilia is defined as sexual perversion in which children (usually before reaching the age of puberty) are a preferred sexual object.[9] This accusation is inaccurately levied against the Prophet (PBUH) for many reasons. Firstly, the marriage to Ā'isha was consummated upon her reaching pubertal maturity. This occurred 3 years after the initial marriage ceremony was completed, as Ā'isha herself explicitly mentions in numerous narrations.[10] Secondly, the fact the Prophet (PBUH) waited 3 years before consummating the marriage shows a level of self-restraint not found in paedophiles, who generally exhibit uncontrollable sexual urges and impulses. This was further corroborated by Ā'isha herself, who reports that the Prophet (PBUH) was in complete control of his desires unlike anybody else.[11] If this allegation of paedophilia was accurate, then it must be asked why the Prophet (PBUH) did not continue to marry more prepubescent girls. All historical sources detailing biographical accounts of the life of the Prophet (PBUH) show quite the opposite: without exception, all marriages of the Prophet (PBUH) after that to Ā'isha were to widows, many of whom were middle-aged. This marks an even more drawn-out, misleading attempt to criticise the moral standing of the Prophet (PBUH). In doing so, this accusation implicitly associates the label of 'paedophile' with the multitude of philosophical frameworks, societies and legislations that permitted similar unions, as we will shortly discuss.

12

Determining Morality

Morality can be determined in one of two main ways: either through a philosophy that does not claim objectivity, or through a philosophy that does. An example of the former is democracy. Many proponents of democracy acknowledge its limitations. Winston Churchill famously said, "Democracy is the worst kind of government except for all of the others we try from time to time."[12] Note that Churchill was careful not to say that democracy is the only true type of government, but instead refers to it as being the best of a bad bunch. Churchill, though, is not the only democrat to acknowledge the limitations of democracy. Ancient philosophers (such as Plato and Socrates) as well as enlightenment philosophers (such as Alexis De Tocqueville and John Stuart Mill) all acknowledge the limitations of democracy. These include the recognition of the ignorance of the masses, or the exploitative nature of democracy against minorities.[13] The latter is a type of philosophy that attempts to construct ultimate, objective truths. Examples of this include Kantianism and consequentialism. Despite attempting to appeal to universal objective truths, these philosophies have proposed mechanisms that are subjective at best. In other words, since the objectivity of these mechanisms cannot be proven, the results produced are also not considered objective. If the instrument

13

of measurement is uncertain, the object of measurement will also be uncertain. If we take our inquiry to an even more sceptical moral consideration, we may consider the view advanced and developed by the Greek historian Herodotus, who lived in the 5th century BC. Herodotus posits that establishing or identifying morals is intrinsic to one's culture or society, and that each society holds that their customs are best; preferring one culture over another is something unattainable.[14] This concept was popularised and gained traction in the era of postmodernism, which views moral relativism as a suspect construction of post-enlightenment thought. Friedrich Nietzsche (d. 1900) was a major proponent of this particular philosophical thought, arguing that moral facts are subjective and grounded in 'perspective' that do not necessarily mirror reality.[15] Richard Rorty[16] highlights that this view, held by Nietzsche and other proponents of postmodernism such as Michel Foucault and Jacques Derrida, expresses that no *actual* criterion exists of morality, only a socially constructed one.

Outside the confines of academia, it is up to the reader to ponder how one establishes a moral compass. Although we openly profess independent thought, are our thoughts influenced by popularist philosophical narratives? One could claim that ethical relativists have no substantive premise to disparage or raise moral objections to a particular group, culture or individual. Applying this to our case study, a question could be asked of a moral relativist or absolutist:

to what extent are their moral objections based on moral principles ascertained without a shadow of philosophical doubt? The obvious answer to this question leads us to acknowledge the philosophical double standards applied by the recent detractors of Islam. Such detractors forge criticism by creating a pseudo-philosophical case using popular aesthetic judgements cloaked in the garb of certain ethical theories.

A Glimpse into History

From a historical perspective, documented marriage pre-dates Christianity and other major world religions by thousands of years.[17] Observing the constitution of marriage and its governing laws throughout history gives us an insight into the moral code and inclination of people at a given time and culture. Margaret Wade Labarge, Professor of History, notes that before the 1900s, "It needs to be remembered that many medieval widows were not old. Important heiresses were often married between the ages of 5 and 10 and might find themselves widowed while still in their teens."[18]

Similarly, Professors Stephen Smallbone and Richard Wortley state that prior to the 1900s, it was the norm that girls were married young:

"In Medieval and early modern European societies, the age of marriage remained low, with documented cases of brides as young as seven years, although marriages were typically not consummated until the girl reached puberty (Bullough 2004). Shakespeare's Juliet was just 13, and there is no hint in the play that this was considered to be exceptional."[19]

Sir John Comyns (d. 1740) highlights that, according to Scottish law prior to the 1900s:

"[A] woman cannot contrahere sponsalia before her age of seven years. *1 Rol. 343. I. 20.* But by common law, persons may marry at any age. *Co. Lit. 33. A.* And upon such marriage the wife shall be endowed, if the attain the age of nine years, of what whatsoever age her husband be; but not before the age of nine years. *Co. L. 33. A.*"[20]

With respect to post-Enlightenment France, Paula Fass notes that the "age of consent laws rose from as low as ten to between thirteen (France 1863) and sixteen (England and Wales 1885)."[21] Susan Ross points out the history of consent in the British Empire:

"According to British common law during the colonial period, the age of consent was seven. Today we are astounded that girls of this age were assumed to know enough about sex (or about sin) to make such a decision competently."[22]

Edward Wood explains how Baron Thomas de Berkeley (d. 1321) was initially due to wed a girl of 7 years old, with consummation of the marriage due to occur 4 years later:

> "Thomas, Lord Berkeley, was contracted to Margaret, daughter of Gerald Warren, Lord Lisle, in the forty-first year of Edward III; and by reason of her tender age - she was then only about seven years old."[23]

English common law allowed individuals to enter a contract of marriage at the age of puberty. This was generally seen as 14 for males and 12 for females.[24] Thus, marriage with females below the age of 16 was accepted in accordance with English law. This was also practised by the British monarchy itself. For example, Lady Margaret Beaufort (d. 1509), the mother of King Henry VII and paternal grandmother of King Henry VIII of England, married John De La Pole (d. 1492) at the age of 7.[25] Similarly, Ann de Mowbray (d. 1481), Duchess of York and Duchess of Norfolk, married when she was 6 years old.[26]

In reference to America, Professor of Sociology Anthony Cortese notes that a 50-year-old man engaging in intimacy with a child under United States law was legal until the mid-1960s:

> "In 1962, the American Law Institute recommended that the legal age of consent to sex - that is, the age below which sex is defined as statutory rape - be dropped in every state to age 10

17

(Katchadourian and Lund 1972: 439). In fact, until the mid-1960s, the legal age of consent in Delaware was 7 (Kling, 1965: 216). So a 50 year old man could legally have sexual intercourse with a 7 year old girl."[27]

This is echoed by Maureen Dabbagh who serves as a Virginia Supreme Court Family Mediator: "[In] the nineteenth century, the minimum age of consent for sexual intercourse in most American states was 10 years. In Delaware it was only 7 years."[28] Furthermore, Professors Smallbone and Wortley mention that "Bullough reports the case in 1689 of a nine-year-old bride in Virginia."[29]

Arthur Siccan presents a historical snapshot of England, Europe and the Western Hemisphere in general:

"Traditionally, across the globe, the age of consent for sexual union was a matter for the family to decide, or a tribal custom. In most cases, this coincided with signs of puberty, menstruation for a woman and pubic hair for a man.

Sir Edward Coke in 17th century England made it clear that the marriage of girls under 12 was normal, and the age at which a girl who was a wife was eligible for a dower from her husband's estate was 9. The American colonies followed the English tradition, and the law was more of a guide. For

18

example, Mary Hathaway of Virginia was only 9 when she was married to William Williams.

Portugal, Spain, Denmark and the Swiss cantons initially set the age of consent at 10-12 years and then raised it to between 13 and 16 years in the second half of the 19th century. Historically, the English common law set the age of consent to range from 10-12. In the United States, by the 1880s, most states set the age of consent at 10-12, and in one state, Delaware, the age of consent was only 7. Social and resulting legal attitudes toward the appropriate age of consent have drifted upwards in modern times. For example, while ages from 10 to 13 were typically acceptable in Western countries during the mid-19th century, the end of the 19th century and beginning of the 20th century were marked by changing."[30]

A Turning Point

An important question remains unanswered: when and why did the age of consent (and thereafter the age of marriage) change in law? The historical turning point could be said to be the Age of Marriage Act 1929 in the United Kingdom, enacted in response to a campaign by the National Union of Societies for Equal Citizenship. The Act raised the minimum age to 16 for both sexes, which remains to this day, as per the Age of Marriage Bill.[31] It is important to recognise that this Act was put in place by a liberal government who had a development plan in the post-WWI period that included educational reform. The interesting point to note here is that the age of consent (which is naturally associated with the age of adulthood) was a historical development initiated by both the economic needs and social pressures after WWI. This is especially the case considering the traction feminist groups had been able to build up, especially by the end of the 20th century and, even more significantly, after universal suffrage Acts were passed. In addition, the events of the Industrial Revolution (which saw a rise in child mortality) was still fresh in the historical memory of the populace. For example, 57% of the working-class children of Manchester died before their fifth birthday [32] and hence a sense of remorse and regret permeated society. Notwithstanding, perhaps one of the most influential exposures in recent times was carried out by the *Pall Mall Gazette*, an evening newspaper in London. In 1885, the newspaper published "The Maiden Tribute of Modern Babylon,"[33] an investigation that alleged that a number of white, virgin girls had become "white slaves" forced into sex slavery. These factors arguably provoked and pushed British legislators to raise the age of consent. It also moved campaigners in the U.S., such as the Women's Christian Temperance Union,[34] to push for similar legislation from governments, which would not be led by resistance from the populace.

The Mind of a Child?

From a physiological perspective, the notion of 'adolescence' throughout history was based on pubertal maturation.[35] This very concept of adolescence is both a mystery and a challenge. What defines adolescence? Is it limited to a set number of biological indicators, or does it encompass social transitions and responsibilities such as marriage and parenthood?[36] What role does neurodevelopmental change play in the determination of adolescence? Many psychologists have reported that in addition to the inextricable link between these factors, the psychological development of a person is itself dependent on environmental influences that differ between cultures and societies. Perhaps the most important influences on psychological development include the social values, norms, and the changing roles, responsibilities, relationships, and expectations of this period of life.[37] The concept of marriage age universally changed during the 20th century in Britain and the U.S. This was due to the colonial power of the British Empire before WWII and the hegemonic power of the U.S. after this period (and specifically after the Cold War). Notions of adulthood, as understood by the English-speaking white person, would quickly spread to the rest of the world. This is generally the trend, although in India (a British colony), the age of consent was adjusted before Britain had formally adjusted its own age of consent.

A rather facetious remark made by Margoliouth was that *'Ā'isha* was "snatched away from her toys". This quip was linked with the ample evidence from the Hadith literature suggesting that *'Ā'isha* played with 'toys' for some time after her marriage to the Prophet (PBUH). However, is the keeping and subsequent usage of dolls and the like inextricably linked to one's psychological maturity? If so, recent studies show an increase in the number of white, conservative, Christian women who actively collect handmade dolls of newborn babies.[38] Additionally, research conducted by the market research company NPD Group shows an increase in the purchase of toys by adults, by almost two-thirds in recent times and over 20% in the last year alone.[39] Is the psychological maturity of these women now in question? Are any of their marital relations untenable and called into dispute?

Appendix 1 details the age of consent in approximately 80 countries from 1880 to 2007. In light of the aforementioned legislations and data, it becomes evident that the main problem that detractors of the Prophet's (PBUH) marriage to *'Ā'isha* have fallen into is the attempt to anachronistically superimpose an arbitrary, subjective, 20th century legalistic definition of immorality on a 7th century Arabian society in which marriages of this sort was something completely accepted. The accusation of paedophilia is unsubstantiated from all of the perspectives discussed above.

Amidst the World Religions

An additional question to pose when morally examining the union of the Prophet (PBUH) to *'Ā'isha* concerns the moral and ethical perspective of such unions amongst other world religions. For example, marriage to very young (at times pre-pubescent) girls was something legally accepted in ancient Israel. John Peter Stehelin (d. 1753) cites Rabbi Solomon Itzhaki (d. 1105) in highlighting that Rebecca was three years old when she married Isaac:

> "Rabbi Solomon in his comment on Genesis, says that Rebecca, when she was married to Isaac, was but three Years of Age. His words run thus, 'When Abraham was come from Mount Moria, he received the joyful News of Rebecca. Isaac was at that Time Thirty seven years old; and then did Sarah die. The time, from birth of Isaac to the death of Sarah, was Thirty seven Years, And Sarah was Ninety Years old when Isaac was born; and One Hundred and Twenty Seven Years old when she died: As it is said in Gen 23:1 . Sarah was one hundred and twenty-seven years old. Behold, the Age of Isaac was Thirty Seven Years, at the Time of the Birth of Rebecca.

And when he had waited for her three Years, till she was fit for marriage, he took her to wife.

According to this Account, Rebecca was a very notable Girl at three years of age. But that a girl of three Years old is fit for marriage, is maintained very plainly in the Jewish writings; particularly, in Emek Hamelech, in the following passage, 'our blessed sags, of blessed memory, say, that a female is not fit for marriage, 'till she is arrived at the Age of three years and one day.'"[40]

This is further cited by numerous researchers, such as Jacob Neusner (d. 2016) in his editorial of *A History of the Mishnaic Law of Purities*, [41] Mark A. Ehrlich in his *Encyclopedia of the Jewish diaspora*,[42] and Steven M. Lowenstein in *The Jewish cultural tapestry*.[43]

Furthermore, many Christian scholars maintain that Joseph was 80-90 years old when he married Mary, who was 12-14 years old. Reverend Jeremiah Jones (d. 1724)[44] opines this in his lengthy justification of the acceptance of the Infancy Protevangelion of James by Early Church Fathers as a truthful account of Mary and Joseph's marriage. Moreover, Numbers 31: 17-18 cannot be ignored:

"Now therefore kill every male among the little ones, and kill every woman that hath known man by lying with him. But all

24

the female children that have not known a man by lying with him, keep alive for yourselves."[45]

Reverend Wil Gafney, an Associate Professor of Hebrew Bible, comments on this verse:

> "The 'one woman, one man' relationship of Eve and Adam becomes one man and two women in Genesis 4:19, one man and an untold number of prepubescent girl captives in Numbers 31:18 and in several other texts. It appears that God has left it to humanity to decide who are appropriate intimate partners and under what circumstances."[46]

With a cursory glance at other ancient world religions, we observe that this practice was similarly accepted both legally and religiously. In Hinduism, for example, Georg Buhler (d. 1898) notes that the Manu (a Hindu juristic and religious scripture) mentions that girls should be wed before reaching pubertal maturity.[47] James Hastings (d. 1922) elucidates in his *Encyclopedia of Religion and Ethics* that "later texts give 4 to 6 as the lower (age of marriage) and 8 as the upper limit. There is abundant evidence that these dates were not merely theoretical".[48] In Sikhism, Guru Gobind Singh (the last of the ten saints) married a 12-year-old girl called Mata Sundari.[49]

Are these practices now seen as repugnant or at odds with current day customs? Perhaps, more candidly, have Judeo-Christian and

Hindu Scholars classified these specific texts as morally and socially decrepit?

An *Usūlī* Perspective

Considering this matter from a strictly Islamic perspective, what would stop (besides the law) a Muslim man or woman above the legal age in Britain from marrying and consummating a marriage with someone below the age of consent? The answer to this question depends on an Islamic *Usūlī* definition of 'harm' that is itself established through specialists from other sciences. We must first caveat this discussion with a preliminary discussion on harm. Harm may be easily categorised into two distinct subsections: that of the body, and the mind. However, does the psychological health of a person exist in a sociological vacuum or does it depend on their environment? What may be considered sociologically normal in one area may be psychologically detrimental in another. If pre-teen marriage was the normative sociological position for earlier societies, what evidence is there that this had a mass impact on the collective psychologies of people? Were societies steeped in such mass ignorance of what would otherwise be easily and empirically identifiable? Compared to most of the major ancient world religions, and most major ideologies, Islam has placed stringent restrictions on marriage to young people who would be otherwise harmed by it.

From a Sunni *Uṣūlī* perspective, harm, or *dharar*, can be either physical, psychological, or monetary. These categories are determined by the cultural norms of a particular time. Since harm is dependent on time and place, and psychological harm of a 9 year-old today is different from that nearly 14 centuries ago, the Islamic ruling would therefore be different. It could be said that the union with pre-teens is forbidden, or *harām*, unless the legal landscape shifts back to pre-1929. This is in accordance with the important juristic legal maxim (*qā'idah fiqhiyyah*) of 'harm is to be removed' (*al-Dharar yuzāl*). The broad understanding of harm according to scholars today includes that of the physical and psychological nature (as mentioned by *al-Munāwi*)[50]. In fact, *al-Shātibī* (d. 790 AH) codifies this concept in his magnum opus *al-Muwāfaqāt*, in which he presents a detailed discussion on the Higher Objectives of the *Shar'īah*: "We have categorically, undeniably extrapolated from the *Shar'īah* that it has been placed for the benefit of mankind."[51] Muhammad Abu Zahrah (d. 1974) comments on these objectives:

> "The defining principle (within the *Shar'īah*) is that any harm is to be warded off, as long as it can be avoided, as the safeguarding of man and preventing harm from befalling upon him, in any way whatsoever, is a firm, established principle in Islam."[52]

"All of the legalistic, juristic rulings are built upon achieving the benefits of the slaves (of Allah) and every established right is stipulated with avoiding any harm."[53]

Thus, it is not in the interests of Muslims to break the long hand of the law in Britain (or any other Western country) not only because of the harms/*mafāsid* that might accrue from this but also because of the general Islamic impermissibility of going against the law.

In Her Own Words

Implicit in the accusations against the union of the Prophet (PBUH) with *Ā'isha* is the inference that *Ā'isha* herself was displeased throughout and was subdued to forcefully accept the marriage. The assumption is that she lived a miserable life in this 'forced' union. Can this outrageous claim be historically substantiated? If any of the claims of the popular detractors had any truth behind them, it can be expected that some substantial evidence for these baseless allegations would surface after the passing of the Prophet (PBUH), at a time when *Ā'isha* would be free to speak without fear of repercussions. Moreover, *Ā'isha* was unique in the fact that she wielded considerable military might in the subsequent turmoil and friction that transpired between the Companions, having commanded an entire army at her will. *Ā'isha* ranks as one of the most knowledgeable of the Companions of the Prophet (PBUH) and is regarded as one of the most prolific narrators of *ahādīth*, having narrated over 2210 hadiths.[54] It is as *al-'Aynī*, the renowned commentator on *Sahīh al-Bukhāri*, remarks, "a quarter of the legalistic judicial rulings present in the *Shar'īah* is by way of *Ā'isha.*"[55] *Ā'isha* was outspoken and was known for her brazenness and audacity in voicing her thoughts, however inconvenient and untimely they may seem. This was all whilst the Prophet (PBUH) was alive, let alone after his passing.

Ā'isha was married to the Prophet (PBUH) for 13 years and continued her scholarly undertakings until she passed away 45 years later. Numerous *ahādīth* narrated by *Ā'isha* herself contend the outlandish remarks against the Prophet (PBUH) and provide incredible insight into a marriage adorned with the utmost respect, dignity, love, and affection. *Ā'isha* narrates: "The Prophet (PBUH) would pass to me a drinking vessel. I would then drink from it, whilst in a state of mensuration, then pass it back to him and he would drink from the same exact spot, searching for the place my lips touched."[56] She also narrates moments that the Prophet (PBUH) enjoyed with her, such as the instance in which the Ethiopians were playing in the mosque and, when she wished to observe them, the Prophet (PBUH) covered her with his cloak and stood there with her until she requested to leave. *Ā'isha* also narrates that the Prophet (PBUH) would often recline in her lap and recite the *Qur'ān.*[57] As a summary of the lofty benchmark in which she held the Prophet's character, she described it by saying that "His character was the *Qur'ān.*"[58]

Conclusion

This article has demonstrated the fallacious and defective reasoning of those who accuse the Prophet Muhammad (PBUH) of depravity and exploitation with respect to his marriage with *Ā'isha*. The article has illustrated the corrigibility (and even the axiomaticity) of the epistemology of Western tradition. The article has also shown that many Western countries legalised or accepted norms that are repugnant to current day Western morality. By looking at the position of opposing schools in philosophy and morality as presented in the ancient major world religions, it becomes obvious that detractors are anachronistic in their historical judgements. This constitutes a fallacy known as the 'fallacy of presentism'. This article is not calling for a reconsideration of the age of consent as (from an Islamic *Usūlī* perspective) harm is reassessed depending on time, place and circumstance. However, the question remains: why should we pass certain moral judgements using moralities that have uncertain moral foundations?

Appendix 1

Table 1. Age Limit in Age of Consent Laws in Selected Countries.
Reproduced from Children and Youth in History, Item #24.
[Online]. Available: http://chnm.gmu.edu/cyh/items/show/24
(Accessed September 21, 2018).

	1880	1920	2007
Austria	14	14	14
Belgium	-	16	16
Bulgaria	13	13	14
Denmark	12	12	15
England & Wales	13	16	16
Finland	-	12	16
France	13	13	15
Germany	14	14	14
Greece	-	12	15
Italy	-	16	14
Luxembourg	15	15	16
Norway	-	16	16
Portugal	12	12	14
Romania	15	15	15

Russia	10	14	16
Scotland	12	12	16
Spain	12	12	13
Sweden	15	15	15
Switzerland	-	16	16
Turkey	15	15	18
Argentina	-	12	13
Brazil	-	16	14
Chile	20	20	18
Ecuador	-	14	14
Canada	12	14	14
Australia			
New South Wales	12	16	16
Queensland	12	17	16
Victoria	12	16	16
Western Australia	12	14	16
United States			
Alabama	10	16	16
Alaska		16	16
Arizona	12	18	18

Arkansas	10	16	16
California	10	18	18
Colorado	10	18	15
Connecticut	10	16	16
District of Columbia	12	16	16
Delaware	7	16	16
Florida	10	18	18
Georgia	10	14	16
Hawaii			16
Idaho	10	18	18
Illinois	10	16	17
Indiana	12	16	16
Iowa	10	16	16
Kansas	10	18	16
Kentucky	12	16	16
Louisiana	12	18	17
Maine	10	16	16
Maryland	10	16	16
Massachusetts	10	16	16
Michigan	10	16	16

Minnesota	10	18	16
Mississippi	10	18	16
Missouri	12	18	17
Montana	10	18	16
Nebraska	10	18	17
Nevada	12	18	16
New Hampshire	10	16	16
New Jersey	10	16	16
New Mexico	10	16	17
New York	10	18	17
North Carolina	10	16	16
North Dakota	10	18	18
Ohio	10	16	16
Oregon	10	16	18
Pennsylvania	10	16	16
Rhode Island	10	16	16
South Carolina	10	16	16
South Dakota	10	18	16
Tennessee	10	18	18
Texas	10	18	17

Utah	10	18	16
Vermont	10	16	16
Virginia	12	16	18
Washington	12	18	16
West Virginia	12	16	16
Wyoming	10	16	16

4:34 - *Qiwāmah, Obedience* & 'Wife-beating'

Introduction

Qiwāmah, as defined in the classical Arabic lexicons, originates from the verbs *qāma* and *yaqumu,* and the verbal nouns *qawm, qiyām,* and *qāmah.* The subject is referred to as *qa'im,* or *qawwām* if the action is emphasised. Linguistically, medieval and classical Arabic dictionaries have defined the meaning of this word in this particular form to embody a combination of protection, sustenance and preservation.[59] Ibn al-Manthur states that the meaning of such a construct is taken from the saying:

> *Qumtu bi amrika* or I have attended to your affair, and as such it is as if the meaning is that men are responsible for the affairs of women, appointed to tend to their affairs and needs.[60]

Other linguistic meanings include standing (or *qiyām*),[61] appropriateness of management,[62] leadership (or al-siyādah,[63] justice and resoluteness,[64] orderliness, regulation, and bearing burdens.[65]

Furthermore, a number of usages are present in the Qur'an, such as *"wa aqīmu al-salāh",* which means to establish and perform the prayer. Likewise, where it is mentioned, *"wa la tu'tu al-sufahā amwālakum allati ja'al Allahu lakum qiyāman",* the intended meaning would be to not bestow the wealth one has been given by Allah upon the foolish, the wealth primarily serving as a means of sustaining oneself[66]. A preliminary examination of the Qur'an

37

shows that the word *qiwāmah* and its derivatives have been used in one hundred and twenty verses, over sixty-three chapters. Exactly thirty-eight of these chapters are Meccan, and twenty-five are Medinan. The presence of *qiwāmah* with its socio-familial meanings are present more in the Medinan chapters. Moreover, the word appears in over 13 different morphological forms.

As for verse 4:34, which has caused great dissatisfaction amongst leading figureheads of modern Islamic feminist thought, the word *qiwāmah* has been used in the subjective form. Through a meticulous analysis of the classical definitions offered by jurists and exegetes, we find that the meaning and general presuppositions of *qiwāmah* differs from the early Qur'anic exegetes to that generally held by the later ones. The early scholars, or *mutaqaddimun*, held that *qiwāmah* revolved predominately around authority, admonition (*ta'dib*), instruction, and legal guardianship[67]. The later exegetes, including modern scholars, generally viewed the meaning of *qiwāmah* to be consistent with protection, management, and maintenance[68]. It should be noted that whilst these meanings are present within the Arabic language, the hermeneutical preferences of each period are indicative of environmental and sociopolitical factors, which undoubtedly influence the respective technical and exegetical position of the scholar.

Why has *Qiwāmah* been instituted on men?

One may question the reasons for which *qiwāmah* has been instituted on men rather than women. Our enquiry leads use to two possible overarching explanations: the first being that which is naturally ordained viz. the natural disposition of the sexes, and the other being an acquisitioned form due to the inherent differences in both sexes. With regards to the first explanation, the common supposition is *kamāl al-'aql*, or perfectness and completeness in the ability to have emotional restraint. This position has been adopted by a host of early exegetes, who refer to the same verse (4:34) in which Allah says, "By right of what Allah has given, one over the other." These early exegetes include Ibn al-'Arabi (d. 543 H)[69], Ibn 'Atiyyah (d. 541 H)[70], al-Zamakhshari (d. 538 H)[71], al-Tha'labi (d. 427 H)[72], al-Baghdadi (d. 741 H)[73], al-Qurtubi (d. 656 H)[74], and al-Jalalain[75]. It should be noted that this concept of completeness of reason has been further interpreted by al-Qurtubi (d. 656 H), al-Māwardi (d. 450 H)[76], and a few others to mean that which arises due to the presence of additional causes naturally occurring in men and thus not found in females, such as intellectual fortitude and strength. Whilst this *tafsīr* has been adopted by some modern exegetes, it appears to be one devoid of any textual evidence. Moreover, since it seemingly contradicts and opposes fundamental legalistic ethics and principles, it could well become void as it necessitates injustice on the part of women.

Illustrating this point further, jurists typically accept that Allah has addressed both sexes in the Qur'an with the same injunctions, unless one sex has been singled out over the other with the presence of a *mukhassis*, or specifying evidence. The Prophet (PBUH) said, "Women are the equal partners of men." [77] This is general in all aspects of both theological and jurisprudential rulings. Claiming that men are more complete in their intellectual aptitude would then result on *ahkām* (rulings) that present a degree of undue liability on the part of women. From a spiritual aspect, both the Qur'an and the *Sunnah* makes plentiful references to piety in the sight of Allah as being the measure of difference and preference:

> O you who believe! be not forward in the presence of Allah and His Messenger, and be careful of (your duty to) Allah; surely Allah is Hearing, Knowing. (Hujurāt:13)

Others have suggested that completeness of religious commitment, or *deen*, is another naturally ordained reason for the institution of *qiwāmah* being apportioned to men.[78] This has been interpreted to mean the increased weightiness of testimony from men compared to women, the obligation of *jumu'ah* prayers on men, and differences in inheritance shares between men and women. This view would also necessitate inequality in legalistic (*shar'i*) injunctions. These topics are further addressed in another paper. It is in line with traditionalist views that postulate that both sexes are alike in their foundational obligations and rights, as well as their reward and recompense, despite each sex being ordained with different responsibilities in line with their respective sex.

Hadith of 'Deficiencies' & Women's Testimony (*Shahādah*)

Common reference is given, both by traditionalists and common Orientalist detractors alike, to the hadith, narrated on the authority of 'Abdullah b. 'Umar, in which the Prophet (PBUH) says, "I have not seen any women lacking in in the ability to have emotional restraint (*nāqisat 'aql*) and religiousness (*nāqisat dīn*) but (at the same time) more able to rob the wisdom of the wise, except one of you [women]." The women the Prophet (PBUH) was addressing asked, "How are we lacking in religious commitment and reason, O Messenger of Allāh?" He replied, "Is not the testimony of a woman like half the testimony of a man?" They said, "Yes." He said, "That is how she is lacking in reason. And when she menstruates, does she not refrain from praying and fasting?" They said, "Yes." He said, "That is how she is lacking in religious commitment."[79]

The question of what constitutes the *'aql* (intellect) is pertinent. Numerous etymological definitions may be accessed from classical sources, ranging from *habs* (a type of constriction)[80], to the antonym of ignorance[81], and, most importantly, rationality.[82] In the context of this hadith, it is assumed that a reference to the ability to control

41

one's emotions is inferred. The general description of women as more 'emotional' than men may seem controversial at the point of description, but this is not so even in second-wave feminism, where modern Western criticism may be directed. As we will come to see, most 'modern day' Euro-American criticism of second-wave feminism is more specifically directed at the point of prescription. Leading second-wave figurehead Simone de Beauvoir writes:

> Overlapping women's specifically sexual differentiations are the singularities, more or less the consequences of these differentiations; these are the hormonal actions that determine her soma. On average, she is smaller than man, lighter; her skeleton is thinner; the pelvis is wider, adapted to gestation and birth; her connective tissue retains fats, and her forms are rounder than man's; the overall look: morphology, skin, hair system, and so on is clearly different in the two sexes. Woman has much less muscular force: about two-thirds that of man; she has less respiratory capacity: lungs, trachea, and larynx are smaller in woman; the difference in the larynx brings about that of the voice. Women's specific blood weight is less than men's: there is less haemoglobin (sic) retention; women are less robust, more apt to be anemic (sic). Their pulse rate is quicker, their vascular system is less stable: they blush easily. Instability is a striking characteristic of their bodies in general; for example, man's calcium metabolism is stable; women both

retain less calcium salt and eliminate it during menstruation and pregnancy; the ovaries seem to have a catabolic action concerning calcium; this instability leads to disorders in the ovaries and in the thyroid, which is more developed in a woman than in a man: and the irregularity of endocrine secretions acts on the peripheral nervous system; muscles and nerves are not perfectly controlled. More instability and less control make them more emotional, which is directly linked to vascular variations: palpitations, redness, and so on; and they are thus subject to convulsive attacks: tears, nervous laughter, and hysterics. [83]

Though it is beyond the scope of this paper to delve deeply into the undergirds of de Beauvoir's existential political philosophy, it may be said that the assumption by second-wave feminism is that, despite such physical and physiological differences between the two sexes, there should be a kind of absolute equality. Although Islamic traditionalism has some notion of gender equality in general, as we have discussed, it does not concur with this notion of equality despite all differences.

Following standard hadith nomenclature (*mustalah*), the hadith mentioned above is amongst the most authentic since it is found in the hadith compilations of both Bukhari and Muslim. Despite attempts by some at weakening it, the hadith does not contain any hidden defect ('*illah*) or non-conformity (*shuthuth*), nor any other cause of weakness in either the chain of transmission or the text of the hadith (*matn*). The context in which the hadith was narrated was in the 'Eid festival, as explicitly mentioned in the particular narration of this hadith by Abu Sa'id al-Khudri. It is farfetched to believe that degradation of any sex over the other was intended as this event occurred in a jovial setting, let alone without a meaning intended to spiritually guide and empower women. In other words, the innate influence that some women have can exert and potentially influence even the shrewdest of people, and as such, this should be used in an ethical, pleasing manner to the Creator in line with Islamic teachings.[84] The question remains: how do we understand the incompleteness (both rational and religious) mentioned in the hadith? In light of the aforementioned principles and legalistic framework of the Sharī'ah according to traditionalist Islam, one can surmise that an acceptable understanding is that the incompleteness is of a temporary, short-term, and specific nature. This incompleteness is one that arises due to specific conditions, as mentioned by the Prophet (PBUH) himself in the hadith. Understood in this light, the incompleteness of rationality is one that is associated with the adjudication of rights, as well as transactions associated with property and wealth:

> ...but if there are not two men, then one man and two women
> from among those whom you choose to be witnesses, so that if

one of the two errs, the second of the two may remind the other. (Baqarah:282)

It should be noted that this commonly quoted verse refers to *ishhād*, or witnessing the exchange of money and property in case of a future dispute. This is different to *shahādah*, which takes place due to former disputes and occurs at the bequest of a judge. Ibn al-Qayyim (d. 751 H) mentions this difference in his manual of judicial methods, *al-Turuq al-Hukmiyyah:*

> There is nothing in the Qur'an which suggests that a ruling must only be passed with two witnesses, or a male and two females, as Allah has only commanded those possessing rights (wealth, etc.) in order to preserve them. He has not, conversely, ordained for judgements to be passed in this manner, let alone restrict it to this. For this reason, a judge may pass judgment via numerous means: a refusal to swear an oath, rejected oaths, a single woman's testimony.[85]

Ibn al-Qayyim also stresses this difference between *shahādah* and *ishhād* by stating that the evidence admissible in court is in fact greater and more diverse than testimony alone:

> Admissible evidence in the Sharī'ah (known as *bayyinah*) can sometimes be three or four witnesses, two witnesses, a single male witness, a single woman's testimony, a refusal to take

oath, singular oaths, at times fifty oaths, four oaths. The statement of the Prophet (PBUH): "The onus (*bayyinah*) is upon the plaintiff" means that upon him is to present that which will verify the validity of his oath, and if ascertained, judgment will be passed in his favour.[86]

In this particular instance, the *'illah* (*ratio legis*) underpinning this difference in the *ishhād* of women and men is one that is of an *ijtihadi* (speculative) nature due to the absence of textual or consensual evidences. However, recent studies have shown a direct correlation between forgetfulness (referred to as such by many of the exegetes) and pregnancy. In a study carried out by Julie Henry and Peter Rendell, they concluded that pregnant women are significantly impaired on some measures of memory [87]. Hence, the verse takes this and other such situations into consideration by providing an effective auxiliary in the form of another woman. Medieval Qur'anic exegetes such as Al-Rāzi (d. 606 H) have posited that this difference is due to biological inferiority, an assertion that is not being made in this paper. Drawing upon Hellenistic physiology, first outlined by Hippocrates (d. 377 BC), he makes this ontological claim "due to the presence of moisture and coldness in their bodies."[88] This is echoed by numerous other exegetes. Other studies have shown that both men and women often recall information in different ways, rather than one being superior over the other. For example, Elizabeth Lotfus reports that accuracy in recall differs depending on the "differential interest in particular items and corresponding differential amounts of attention paid to those items."[89] In other words, the sociocultural milieu affects the ability to recall certain items over others. We will return to this point shortly.

Hadith Narration (*Riwāyah*)

Drawing a comparison between testimony and hadith narration, there appears to be no dissimilarity between males and females, despite the importance and brevity of these actions. Al-Hāfith al-'Irāqi (d. 806 H) formalises the conditions of an authentic hadith in his *Alfiyyah* (a versification of Ibn al-Salah's magnum opus, *An Introduction to the Science of Hadith*):

And the first (category) is a connected chain of transmission

By the one who is trustworthy ('adl) and reliable (dhābit).[90]

The two prerequisite conditions for the acceptance of a narrator was their *'adālah* (trustworthiness) and *'dhabt* (reliability). This gender neutrality been echoed throughout the centuries in hadith sciences, and has been taken as near consensus. There were many prolific hadith narrators who were women, chief of which was the Prophet Muhammad's (PBUH) wife 'Aisha, who was amongst the most prolific of the companions who have narrated this important source of legislation. Recent research by In his voluminous work *al-*

Muhaddithāt: The Women Scholars in Islam, Akram Nadwi outlines the biographies of over eight thousand women scholars of hadith.[91] Amazingly, the 8th century historian Imam al-Thahabi (d. 748 H) said, "I am unaware of a single woman who narrates hadith that has been accused of lying, nor one who has been rejected due reliability."[92] A similar statement has been reported by the 8th century hadith scholar Ibn Hajr (d. 852 H).[93]

The question may be asked: what led to the demarcation between hadith narration and *shahādah* with respect to women? One immediately notes that there does not exist a consensus amongst Islamic scholars as to the cause of this binary division. Some scholars seemingly understood this point and inferred that the sociocultural milieu may have played an active role in determining whether plurality in women's testimony was indeed a requirement. In his seminal work *I'lam al-Muwaqqi'in*, Ibn al-Qayyim (d. 751 H) asserts that if a woman could prove herself to be trustworthy and dependable in other areas, then her testimony should be accepted, irrespective of the area:

> If a woman is credible and trustworthy in her religiosity, then the intended objective has been reached with her testimony, and as such, her lone testimony is accepted in certain places.[94]

In his magnum opus on Islamic judicial law, Ibn Qudāmah (d. 620 H) states various scenarios in which a woman's singular testimony is accepted over a man's due to these scenarios being generally more attended and witnessed by females:

> (A woman's lone testimony) is accepted in that which men are not usually privy to, such as issues connected to breastfeeding, childbirth, menses, *'iddah*, and affairs similar to these. We do not know of any difference of opinion amongst the scholars regarding this.[95]

Thus, the question of whether the *ratio legis* of verse 2:228 was based on a prevalent sociocultural or economical milieu is still present and argued strongly by numerous scholars such as Ibn Taymiyyah and Ibn al-Qayyim.

Qiwāmah - Financial Responsibility

With regard to the acquisitioned (*kasbi*) reason behind the institution of *qiwāmah* on men, we are directed to next part of the same verse, in which Allah says: "And due to that which they spend, from their wealth." *Qiwāmah* is thus described as being of an economical nature, an obligation on the husband to tend to the general financial responsibilities of the household. Many jurists have explicitly ruled that if this financial responsibility cannot be met, it is within the remit of the wife to demand an annulment of the marriage from the relevant authorities, since *qiwāmah* would no longer be present. This view is held by the majority of the juristic schools of thought: the Hanābilah,[96] the Shāfi'iyyah,[97] and the

49

Mālikiyyah.[98] This is perhaps one of the single most important rights of the wife in the institution of marriage.

Obedience (*Tā'ah*)

A common central meaning of the verse espoused by exegetes across the centuries surrounds the concept of *tā'ah*. Qādhi Ibn al-'Arabi (d. 543 H), a 6th century exegete and Māliki jurist, defined *qiwāmah* as, "Being entrusted with her [i.e. the wife's] wellbeing, addressing her affairs, rectifying that which requires correction, as mentioned by Ibn 'Abbas [d. 68 H], and that *tā'ah* is incumbent upon her, towards him [i.e. the husband]."[99] Likewise, similar explanations are offered by other exegetes such as al-Jassās (d. 370 H), al-Qurtubī (d. 671 H) , al-Shawkāni (d. 1255 H), and al-Tha'labi (d. 427 H) among many others.[100] It could thus be inferred that this is the majority opinion, if not a consensual one. It should be noted that this is understanding of a Qur'anic phrase is by a Companion of the Prophet (PBUH), and as such has a strong authority within the normative exegetic tradition, especially if there is no known opposing view within other Companions. Al-Tabari (d. 310 H) narrates from Ibn 'Abbas (d. 68 H):

> *Qawamuna 'ala al-nisa*, meaning, men are *umarā* (leaders); upon her is to embody *tā'ah* towards him in that which Allah

has ordained upon her. *Tā'ah* towards him entails that she does well by his family and guards his wealth.[101]

What is *tā'ah*? How has the Sharī'ah and juristic tradition defined this concept and apportioned the rulings between genders? What are its confines and limits?

Tā'ah is defined lexically to mean *inqāda*, or to acquiesce willingly.[102] Contextualising this, therefore, entails that this acquiescence or acceptance from the wife is one done willingly and out of respect and admiration as ordained by the *qiwāmah* of the husband. It should be noted that *tā'ah* is not something constricted only to marital hierarchy, but rather something that transcends any intra-creational interaction. It is something paramount first and foremost with the Creator:

> O you who believe! Obey Allah and obey the Messenger and those in authority from among you; then if you quarrel about anything, refer it to Allah and the Messenger, if you believe in Allah and the last day; this is better and very good in the end. [4:59]

In the spirit of this verse, whoever has an authority over something is to be afforded obedience in that respect, "including the obedience of a wife to her husband."[103] This is also inferred from verse 4:34, in which Allah uses the term *qānitāt* (feminine plural) to describe the inter-spousal *tā'ah* dynamic. Many exegetes have explained that this

51

word, which originates from the verb *qanata* (to observe, obey, and conform), means that general obedience is incumbent upon wives towards their husbands in that which is legislated, as stated by al-Tha'labi (d. 427 H) and others.[104]

The Sharī'ah has precisely defined the remits and confines of this authority in that which is not in direct contravention to divine commandments and prohibitions, hence setting this as the default position. The Prophet (PBUH) said, "Obedience is not valid if it involves sin,"[105] as well as, "Indeed, obedience is only in the good."[106] These *ahaadith* also represent agreed-upon legal maxims held by jurists across different traditions. Hence, if a husband requests of his wife that which infringes on her responsibilities towards Allah, then compliance is not only non-obligatory, but also sinful. Understanding this allows for further introspection as to when and where obedience of the husband is paramount. Furthermore, the inbuilt flexibility of the Sharī'ah further determines and safeguards the wife from obedience of that which is deemed an intrusion of her rights, such as a direct request for financial support in what should be the responsibility of the husband (see above). Moreover, not only does the Sharī'ah stipulate obedience to be in that which is permitted, it also places restrictions on that which may present harm, subject to the legal maxim 'harm is to be removed' (*al-Dharar yuzāl*). According to the normative Sunni *(Usuli)* position, harm (*dharar*) can be physical, financial, and psychological (determined by professionals and accepted authorities). The broad understanding of harm according to scholars today includes that of the physical and psychological (as mentioned by al-Munāwi).[107] Al-Shāṭibī (d. 790 AH) codifies this concept in his magnum opus *al-Muwāfaqāt*, in which he presents a detailed discussion on the 'Higher Objectives' of the Sharī'ah: "We have categorically, undeniably extrapolated from the Sharī'ah that it has been placed for the benefit of mankind."[108] Muhammad Abu Zahrah (d. 1974) comments on these objectives:

> The defining principle (within the Sharī'ah) is that any harm is to be warded off, as long as it can be avoided, as the safeguarding of man and preventing harm from befalling upon him, in any way whatsoever, is a firm, established principle in Islam.[109]

> All of the legalistic, juristic rulings are built upon achieving the benefits of the slaves (of Allah) and every established right is stipulated with avoiding any harm.[110,111]

Al-Tabari (d. 310 H) comments on the verse in 2:228: 'and the men are a degree above them, and Allah is Mighty, Wise', by saying:

> And the preferred opinion amongst the many mentioned is what Ibn 'Abbas referred to, which was that Allah has placed additional responsibility upon men in order for them to discharge the rights that women have upon them.[112]

53

One would reasonably expect Euro-centric second-wave feminism approaches to dismiss this kind of husband-wife interaction as against 'equality'. As we have discussed, this rests on the assumption that the physical and psychological differences between men and women should be ignored in social prescription. As discussed by Al-Tabari, 'rights' in Islam are not just seen as existing by themselves in isolation, contrary to liberal individualism. Islamic law traditionally viewed 'responsibilities' as being necessarily conjoined to such rights. In this way, *qiwāmah* is a position of familial responsibility which, if not taken seriously, naturally means that a person may be taken to account for their irresponsibility.

Wife-beating?

The portion of verse 4:34 that Orientalists depict as purportedly encouraging 'wife-beating' is an important discussion. How could the Sharī'ah be opposed to the facilitation of harm yet seemingly enjoin domestic violence? How could the Sharī'ah sanction domestic violence when the Prophet (PBUH) was clear in his aversion to it? It has been reported that the Prophet (PBUH) said, "Hit not the female servants of Allah,"[113] and he was reported to have "had never hit a servant, nor a woman, or indeed, struck anything with his hand."[114]

Traditionally, the word *fadhribuhunna* has been understood by some exegetes and jurists to apply in regulated and strict circumstances, when a husband is granted legal authority to physically discipline their wives. Unqualified, it could be interpreted that a husband has free reign to physically discipline as he likes, without any fear of reprimand. However, the juristic tradition is replete with examples of Muslim judges routinely ruling in favor of physical punishment to be meted out to husbands who have caused physical harm to their wives.[115] Referring back to early exegetical sources, we find that the Meccan jurist and exegete 'Ata b. Abi Rabāh (d. 110 H) interpreted this Qur'anic concept as follows: "A man must not hit his wife - if he instructs her and she does not comply, he should show his anger."[116] Ibn 'Arabi comments:

> This is from the delicate understanding of 'Ata. Due his understanding of the Sharī'ah and deductive ability, he coined that the unrestricted ruling is one of permissibility, downgraded to being disliked (*makruh*) due to the statement of the Prophet (PBUH) from the hadith of 'Abdullah b. Zam'ah: "Indeed I dislike that a man should hit his wife due to his anger and then be intimate with her later on."[117]

Thus, some leading scholars have suggested that these reports collectively indicate that this 'hitting' (*dharb*) is something symbolic, intended to communicate the acute seriousness of the marital discord (*nushuz*)[1] mentioned in the verse. This 'hitting' could be no more than an 'energetic demonstration'[118], although it is utterly disliked by the majority of jurisprudential schools.[119] The principle of averting harm will always maintain that nothing grievous in nature can be permitted, even if a contrasting view is adopted. Moreover, if it is expected that marital discord would not be resolved by way of this *dharb*, then some scholars have declared it to be manifestly impermissible, such as the Māliki jurist al-Hattāb.[120]

'Just Say No'

Metonymical interpretations that effectively render the source text null and void of any textual meaning are the result of various ideological causes and origins. Some of these interpretations hail from a more technical, *Usuli* approach, while others arise from a linguistic, hermeneutical perspective. An example of the latter comes from Asma Barlas, who translated the verse 4:34 to mean 'to hold in confinement'. A frequently-cited participant in the mushrooming Islamic feminist discourse in the last 25 years is Amina Wadud. Whilst she is opposed to the label of 'Islamic feminism'[121], Wadud falls within Badran's definition of "a feminist

---

[1] *Nushuz* has been defined by the various juristic traditionalist schools in multiple ways, ranging from disobedience to committing adultery. For example, the Hanbalis define it as, "Disobedience stemming from the wife in regards to rights of marriage," as described by Ibn Qudāmah in *Al-Kāfī* (3/137).

discourse and practice articulated within an Islamic paradigm … which derives its understanding and mandate from the Qur'an."[122]

Initially, in Wadud's view, this verse acted as a restraint on existing cultural practices that allowed for the unrestricted beating of wives. She argues that the other form of the verb, *darraba*, which is indicative of a more intense striking, was not used. This implies that the striking advocated in the verse is one that is light. However, her recent work titled *Inside the Gender Jihad,* Wadud adopts an outright rejection of the text:

> There is no getting around this one, even though I have tried through different methods for two decades. I simply do not and cannot condone permission for a man to 'scourge' or apply *any kind* of strike to a woman … I have finally come to say 'no' outright to the literal implementation of this passage.[123]

Besides having no jurisprudential precedence, Wadud's interpretation is unacceptable on linguistic and *Usuli* grounds, having no prior precedent within the traditional corpus of Islamic literature. Moreover, it is unclear why Wadud predicates her analysis on second-wave feminist approaches without clear philosophical justification from first-wave feminist principles. Hence, Wadud presents her argument as either morally real or axiomatically objective. Furthermore, she uses a particular strand of feminist theory to represent all of feminist theory, thereby disregarding third-wave, queer, and intersectional feminist analysis. It is clear that Wadud predicates her subsequent hermeneutical approach on the assumption that gender is more important than class, race, or religion. Not only is this somewhat elitist, it is also unproved and unsubstantiated. Finally, Wadud makes no effort to survey or research the attitudes and understandings of women in the 'third world'. Her picture of women is essentialised in the way she presents all women as a monolith, a notion that is antithetical to third-wave feminist and post-structuralist approaches. One may question to what extent do women want to live in societies that are modelled on Western patriarchal societies. How are freedom, equality, and patriarchy defined? Wadud makes no attempt at answering these pressing questions in her discourse.

Conclusion

We have attempted to flesh out some of the key contentions relating to women's rights and responsibilities with reference to the classical Sunni jurisprudence, as well as approaches from second-wave feminism. Although this was not a paper on political philosophy, some mention has been made on the reasons for controversy in the first place, which relates to a Euro-centric second-wave feminism problematisation of the Qur'anic verses and hadith. We have seen that some criticisms of Islamic texts have not taken into consideration the important nuances in jurisprudence between different kinds of testimony, namely, *shahādah*, *ishhād*, and *riwāyah*. The casual conflation and careless combination of these important terms of jurisprudential significance into the single English term 'witness testimony' does not do justice to the classical Islamic positions.

We have discussed the concessions in the Shari'ah for women based on their physical and physiological differences, and we have argued that subsequent prescriptions that differentiate rulings based on such distinguishers are not inconsistent. This paper has not dealt with points of difference in which women have rights and responsibilities not afforded to men. Such a topic requires a separate academic treatment. Finally, this paper has criticised 'modern' approaches such as those promulgated by Amina Wadud. Such attempts are certainly problematic from an intersectional perspective since they do not seek to consult 'third world' women in judging what their most important points of identification are, and make no attempt to enquire from such 'third-world' women on their theory of moral justice. It may be very well the case, confirmed by data from Pew Research,[124] that the majority of such women would conform more to a traditional understanding of 'obedience' than a Euro-centric, Orientalist one. For this reason, Wadud's rendition of the verse for 'moral' reasons is acutely illegitimate from an intersectional analysis, which aims to represent women from the Orient.

Divorce: Are Married Muslim Women 'Trapped'?

Introduction

Orientalist discourse has often presented the image of the married Muslim woman as a trapped and subjugated individual who, for religious reasons, is unable to end a marriage in any circumstance unless the husband 'approves'. While such marriage traps exist within some Jewish contexts (where a woman is required to obtain a *get* from her husband before divorce) and in historical Catholic rulings (where divorce is disallowed for the most part), women in Islam have always had an ability to autonomously obtain a divorce without a husband's 'permission'. Whilst Islam does seek to uphold the sanctity of marriage and avoid divorce if possible, the *Sharī'ah* clearly provides recourse for either spouse to end the marriage if the rights and responsibilities of the marriage are jeopardised or compromised.

Types of Legal Separation in Islam

Various *Fiqhi* (Islamic jurisprudential) works across different schools of thought mention numerous types of legal divorce or separation: *talāq, faskh* (dissolution, sometimes used synonymously with *furqah/tafriq*), and *khul'* (annulment).

Talāq is the most common type of divorce. It is the unilateral right of the husband to initiate, and its effects are immediate. However, the process of finalisation is dependent on the *'iddah*, the respective waiting period endured by the wife, which may be a minimum of a few months to years depending on whether she is pregnant or breastfeeding. This is in stark contrast to *khul'*, which is the wife's right (or indeed, her legal guardian or substitute) to seek the annulment of the marriage in exchange for the dower (*mahr*) to be returned to the husband. The wife reserves the right to initiate the *khul'* and the process of finalisation, due to the *'iddah* being one menstrual cycle (according to numerous jurists).[125] Many jurists have stated that the institution of *khul'* was legislated to protect and preserve the wife from any probable harm, whether psychological or religious. This harm could include either spouse committing immoral and impermissible means to address their desires due to a lack of attraction between the married individuals.[126] Allah says:

> [U]nless both fear that they cannot keep within the limits of Allah; then if you fear that they cannot keep within the limits of Allah, there is no blame on them for what she gives up to become free thereby. These are the limits of Allah, so do not exceed them, and whoever exceeds the limits of Allah then it is they that are the unjust. [2:229]

Interestingly, the majority of jurists explicitly allow a type of *talāq* in which the wife is afforded complete choice and agency on initiation of the process. This is known as *talāq al-tafwidh*. The 7th century Hanbali judge and jurist Ibn Qudāmah discusses this in his encyclopaedic work on Islamic jurisprudence:

> A summary of this issue is that the husband can either initiate the divorce himself, or grant agency to someone else or delegate the choice to his wife. The evidence for this is that the Prophet (PBUH) gave his wives the option of divorce or to remain with him, and they chose to remain with him. Additionally, whenever the *talāq* is granted to be placed under the bequest of the wife, then it remains with her permanently.[127]

Islamic jurists have mentioned numerous reasons to permit *faskh* (dissolution of the marriage contract), ranging from the inability of the husband to financially sustain his wife or to uphold the initially agreed upon dower[128], to extreme cases in which the husband swears an oath to never engage in sexual intimacy with his wife (known as *ilā*).[129]

In most cases, a judge is required to authorize the separation in both *khul'* and *faskh*. However, historical records show that the seemingly unfettered authority granted to men to issue *talāq* was somewhat controlled by the increase in responsibilities for men to fulfill. These responsibilities included monetary support during the *'iddah* (waiting period). Indeed, more ways were provided for women to seek recourse. It was also upon the man to pay in full the agreed dower, as well as cover the expenses of any children involved in the marriage, irrespective of which of the spouses receives custody of the children.

One or Four?

Islam accounts for any sentiment that a potential spouse may feel towards the practise of polygamy. Although this essay does not intend to address the various issues that are mentioned in the popular discourse on polygamy, it intends to display the inbuilt flexibility in treating the unique emotions that a potential spouse may have towards it. The Qur'anic discourse encourages the marriage of only one spouse: "You will never be able to treat your wives equally, however much you may desire to do so" [4:129]. This understanding was held by numerous jurists such as al-Shafi'i (d. 204 H). The majority of jurists allow for a potential female spouse to stipulate in the pre-marriage contract that her husband is not lawfully permitted to practise polygamy while he is married to her. This concern for the feelings of one's spouse was a precedent set by the Prophet (PBUH) himself when he voiced his reason for not marrying a woman from the residents of al-Madinah despite her beauty:

They [i.e. the women of al-Madinah] are women with strong protective jealousy and would not endure a marriage with multiple co-wives, and I would dislike to harm her [i.e. the woman from al-Madinah] people by causing her to be distressed.[130]

Exploitation of minute technicalities in the *Sharī'ah* can be done on both sides, by both husband and wife. An example of this is the process of *tahlil*, which occurs when a divorcee woman – who cannot legitimately remarry her spouse due being divorced three times (known as *baynunah kubra*) – must marry another spouse and consummate the marriage, before then being divorced and thus becoming *halal* (permitted) to remarry her first spouse. Despite being a type of marriage universally prohibited by the majority of jurists, it is commonly practised amongst certain circles. Interestingly, this form of marriage represents a type of polyandrous relationship, as the first husband is ever-present and indeed consenting to this process.

Conclusion

It should be known that Islam is one of the few major world religions that has extensively legislated and protected the interests of the wife in all cases of legal separation. This protection is offered both before and after separation, and provides exhaustive recourse for a woman and her guardian(s) to take in order to separate from her spouse. This is in stark contrast to Christianity, in which the New Testament explicitly mentions only two reasons justifying divorce: adultery (see Matthew 19:9), and when a non-Christian spouse abandons the marriage (see 1 Corinthians 7)[131]. Islam recognises that spouses may not always be compatible and that reconciliation may seemingly be distant. Islam therefore provides multiple solutions for legal separation whilst never demonising either party. This point is clearly illustrated and exemplified in the life of the Prophet (PBUH), who exclusively married divorcees, with the exception of his union with 'Āisha.

Does Islam Favour Men Over Women in Inheritance laws?

Introduction

Linguistically, the word *irth* means a estate that is transferred from person to person. It can also mean 'an aged affair' or 'remnants'. Its technical, jurisprudential meaning has been defined by the Hanbali jurist Afdhal al-Deen al-Khunji as, "A right which can divided to those legislatively entitled to it, after the passing of the deceased, due to *qarābah* (familial closeness) or that which is similar to it."[132] For the most part, the legislative laws that act as the foundation for inheritance are defined in textual sources from both the Qur'an and *ahādith*, leaving little room for any independent interpretation.

The Mechanisms of Islamic Inheritance

The rulings of inheritance observe a number of criteria in determining the allocated shares each party receives. Firstly, the proximity *(qarābah)* or remoteness of the heirs is considered. For example, the daughter of the deceased inherits half the estate than her grandmother would, whereas the deceased's father is entitled to only a fourth. Secondly, the *Sharī'ah* seeks to observe the generational position of the heirs. For example, a daughter will inherit more than her grandmother, yet both are females. Likewise, a daughter will inherit half of her father's estate, whilst the deceased's father is only deserving of the unclaimed remainder of the estate. Thirdly, the financial burden and obligations of the heirs are taken into account. It is this third criteria that results in the usual difference in respective shares. As discussed previously in the meaning of the *qiwāmah*, the financial responsibility upon a husband is considered from amongst the foremost rights of the wife, and indeed the greater family as a whole, including other dependents for whom the man serves as the primary provider. At the same time, the wife is entitled to her husband's wealth (without his permission in certain cases), whereas she has complete autonomy with her own wealth and shares none of the financial responsibilities meted out to the husband.

Down To The Facts

An exhaustive reading (*istiqrā'*) within various jurisprudential compendiums – avoiding minute, valid differences amongst the *mathāhib* – presents the following scenarios of inheritance:

1. There exist only four scenarios in which a female inherits *half* that of a male (of equal position). For example:

    a. The presence of a daughter and a son, or indeed a granddaughter and grandson, in which case the son (or grandson) will inherit twice as much as the daughter (granddaughter), outlined in the verse, "Allah instructs you concerning your children: for

70

the male, what is equal to the share of two females" [4:11].

b. The deceased father and mother being the only inheritors, without spouses or children. Regarding this case, Allah says, "But if he [i.e. the deceased] had no children and the parents (alone) inherit from him, then for his mother is one-third" [4:11]. Thus, one-third is reserved for the mother, whilst the father will receive two-thirds.

2. At least eleven scenarios where a female inherits the **same** share as a male. For example:

a. The inheritance of a mother and father, with the presence of the deceased son. In this case, both the mother and father will inherit one-sixth, whilst the son will receive the remainder of the estate.

b. A scenario termed *al-Mushtarikah*, in which the husband, mother, two maternal sisters, and her full brother remain. The husband will inherit one-half, the mother one-sixth, and both maternal sisters and the full brother will inherit one-third divided equally amongst them.

3. Sixteen scenarios in which a female inherits **more** than a male. This is because Islamic inheritance relies upon two main mechanisms. The first is inheritance via a fixed portion due to specific individuals (providing relevant conditions are fulfilled). This is termed *ashāb al-furudh* and is specified in the Qur'an and Prophetic tradition. These fixed portions are as follows: two-thirds, one-third, one-sixth, one-half, one-quarter, and one-eighth. The second mechanism is inheritance due to other than the specific individuals specified from the *ashāb al-furudh*; these heirs are referred to as *'asabah*. The *'asabah* have no specific share. We can thus deduce the following (notwithstanding the relevant conditions for each type of heir):

   a. The largest share from the fixed portions are two-thirds, and this has been specified for women alone (in specific: four types of women).

   b. Half of an estate is reserved for four types of women, in comparison to only one male (a husband).

   c. One-third is due to two types of women: a mother, and maternal sisters.

   d. One-sixth is due to five types of women and only three types of men.

   e. One-fourth is reserved for a wife and likewise for a husband.

f. One-eighth is also reserved for a wife alone.

Thus, seventeen out of twenty-three fixed portions are due to women and, as shown above, they duly inherit more than males.

4. Five scenarios in which females inherit, and males *do not* inherit anything at all. For example, in the presence of a husband and full sister, the paternal sister will inherit 14.3%, whereas the paternal brother is not entitled to anything.[133]

Conclusion

We have shown that the Islamic laws of inheritance are incredibly detailed and exhaustive. The 19th century professor of law Almaric Rumsey wrote:

> The Moohummudan law of inheritance comprises, beyond question, the most refined and elaborate system of rules for the devolution of property that is known to the civilized world, and its beauty and symmetry are such that it is worthy to be studied, not only by lawyers with a view to its practical application, but for its own sake, and by those who have no other object in view than their intellectual culture and gratification.[134]

This is in stark contrast to the Western tradition in which women in general, and married women in specific, had virtually no right to intestate succession. Until the end of the sixteenth century, women were denied the right to inherit property.[135] The Islamic position is also favourable when compared with other ancient world religions, such as Judaism, in which emphasis is largely placed on the care of the widow, with very few scenarios in which she or other female members have a right to inherit. This is notwithstanding the fact that Islam legislated the inheritance of freed bondsmen and women and ensured their right to the former owner's estate (known as *walā*). This particular area offers an interesting scope for further research, and particularly from the angle of the *maqāsid* (higher aims and objective of the *Sharī'ah*) in inheritance as a whole. It is within the larger picture of the intricate system of Islamic finance that contextualisation represents a vital step towards understanding the rulings of inheritance, rather than superficial and shallow attempts (intentional or not) at representing the breadth and diversity present therein.

References

[1] D. S. Margoliouth, *Mohammed and the Rise of Islam*. New York and London: G. P. Putnam's Sons, 1905.

[2] M. Ibn Sa'd, *Al-Tabaqat al-Kubra*. Beirut: Dar Sadir, 1968, vol 8, p. 59.

[3] S. Ockley, *The History of the Saracens*. London: Henry G. Bohn, 1848.

[4] H. Prideaux. The true nature of imposture fully displayed in the life of Mahomet with a discourse annexed, for the vindication of Christianity from this charge [Online]. Available: http://tei.it.ox.ac.uk/tcp/Texts-HTML/free/A55/A55822.html

[5] E. Gibbon, *The History of the Decline and Fall of the Roman Empire*. London: J. Murray, 1846

[6] I. Goldziher, S. M. Stern, & C. R. Barber, *Muslim Studies*. New

York: State University of New York Press, 1973

[7] G. B. Shaw, *The Genuine Islam*. 1936.

[8] T. Carlyle, *On Heroes, Hero-worship, and the Heroic in History*. California: University of California Press, 1993.

[9] World Health Organisation. ICD Version: 2015 [Online]. Available: http://apps.who.int/classifications/icd10/browse/2015/en#F65.1

[10] M. Nawawi, *Al-Minhaj Sharh Sahih Muslim*. Beirut: Dar Ihya al-Turath al-'Arabi, 1392, vol 9 p. 207.

[11] M. al-Bukhāri, *Saḥīḥ al-Bukhāri*, vol 1, Hadith number 299.

[12] HC Deb. Parliament Bill [Online]. Available: https://api.parliament.uk/historic-hansard/commons/1947/nov/11/parliament-bill

[13] J. Struan, "John Stuart Mill on the tyranny of the majority," *Australian Journal of Political Science*, vol. 28, no. 2, pp. 306-321,

1993.

[14] C. Gowans. Moral Relativism [Online]. The Stanford Encyclopaedia of Philosophy. Available: https://plato.stanford.edu/archives/sum2018/entries/moral-relativism/.

[15] B. Leiter, "Perspectivism in Nietzsche's Genealogy of Morals," in *Nietzsche, Genealogy, and Morality: Essays on Nietzsche's" On the Genealogy of Morals*, R. Schacht Ed. California: University of California Press, 1994.

[16] R. Rorty, *Consequences of Pragmatism*. Minneapolis: University of Minnesota Press, 1982.

[17] J. M. Bowler, H. Johnston, J. M. Olley, J. R. Prescott, R. G. Roberts, W. Shawcross, N. A. Spooner, "New ages for human occupation and climatic change at Lake Mungo, Australia," *Nature*, vol. 421, no. 6925, pp. 837–840, 2003.

[18] M. W. Labarge, *A Medieval Miscellany*. Quebec: McGill-Queen's University Press, 1997, p. 52.

[19] R. Wortley, S. Smallbone, *Internet Child Pornography: Causes, Investigation, and Prevention*. California: Prager, 2012, p. 10.

[20] J. Comyns, A. Hammond, T. Day, *A Digest of the Laws of England*. New York: Collins & Hannay, 1825, vol 2, p. 72.

[21] P. S. Fass. *The Routledge History of Childhood in the Western World*. Abingdon: Routledge, 2013, p. 235.

[22] S. M. Ross, *American Families Past and Present: Social Perspectives on Transformations*. New Jersey: Rutgers University Press, 2006, p. 40.

[23] E. J. Wood. *The Wedding Day in All Ages and Countries*. New York: Harper & Bros, 1869, pp. 209-210.

[24] N. V. Lowe, G. Douglas. *Bromley's Family Law*, 8th ed. Oxford: Oxford University Press, 1992, p. 35.

[25] R. A. Griffiths, *King and Country: England and Wales in the Fifteenth Century*. London: Hambledon Press, 1991, p. 91

[26] D. L. Tunis. *Fast Facts on Kings and Queens of England.* Indiana: Author House, 2005, p. 125.

[27] A. J. P. Cortese. *Opposing Hate Speech.* California: Greenwood Publishing Group, 2006, p. 85.

[28] M. Dabbagh. *Parental Kidnapping in America: An Historical and Cultural Analysis.* North Carolina: McFarland, 2011, p. 128.

[29] R. Wortley, S. Smallbone, *Internet Child Pornography: Causes, Investigation, and Prevention.* California: Prager, 2012.

[30] A. Siccan, *What's Wrong in America.* Indiana: Trafford Publishing, 2012.

[31] HL Deb. The Law of Marriage [Online]. Available: https://www.parliament.uk/about/living-heritage/transformingsociety/private-lives/relationships/overview/lawofmarriage-/

[32] J. Rule, *Labouring Classes in Early Industrial England, 1750-1850.* Abingdon: Routledge, 1986, pp. 87-89.

[33] D. Gorham, "The "maiden tribute of modern Babylon" re-examined: Child prostitution and the idea of childhood in late-Victorian England," *Victorian Studies*, vol. 21, no. 3, pp. 353-379, 1978.

[34] S. Robertson, Age of Consent Laws [Online]. Available: http://chnm.gmu.edu/cyh/items/show/230.

[35] J. Rifkin. *The Empathic Civilization: The Race to Global Consciousness in a World in Crisis.* London: Penguin, 2009.

[36] S. M. Sawyer, P. S. Azzopardi, D. Wickremarathne, G. C. Patton, "The age of adolescence," *The Lancet Child & Adolescent Health*, vol. 2, no. 3, pp. 223-228, 2018.

[37] World Health Organisation. Adolescent development [Online]. Available: http://www.who.int/maternal_child_adolescent/topics/adolescence/development/en/

[38] J. Estrin. (2013, February). "Motherhood, Reborn and Everlasting." *The New York Times* [Online]. Available: https://lens.blogs.nytimes.com/2013/02/19/motherhood-reborn-and-everlasting/

[39] NPD Group. 'Kidults' appetite for toys continues to rise, growing 8% in value in 2017 [Online]. Available: https://www.npdgroup.co.uk/wps/portal/npd/uk/news/press-releases/kidults-appetite-for-toys-continues-to-rise-growing-8-in-value-in-2017/

[40] J. P. Stehelin. *Rabinical Literature: Or, The Traditions Of The Jews, Contained in Their Talmud and Other Mystical Writings.* Robinson, 1748, vol. 1, pp. 33-34.

[41] J. Neusner, *A History of the Mishnaic Law of Purities, Part 21: The Redaction and Formulation of the Order of Purities in Mishnah and Tosefta.* Oregon: Wipf and Stock, 2007, vol. 21, p. 83.

[42] M. A. Ehrlich, *Encyclopedia of the Jewish Diaspora: Origins, Experiences, and Culture.* California: ABC-CLIO, 2009, vol. 1, p. 258.

[43] S. M. Lowenstein, *The Jewish Cultural Tapestry: International Jewish Folk Traditions.* Oxford: Oxford University Press, 2002, p. 108.

[44] J. Jones, *A New and Full Method of Settling the Canonical Authority of the New Testament.* Oxford: Clarendon Press, 1798, vol 2, p. 116.

[45] N. Webster, *The Webster Bible.* Michigan: Baker Publishing Group, 1988.

[46] G. R. Hall, R. A. Meyers, *Christian Holiness and Human Sexuality: A Study Guide for Episcopalians.* London: Church Publishing, 2011.

[47] G. Buhler. *The Laws of Manu.* CreateSpace Independent Publishing Platform, 2016. (See also G. Jha, *Manusmrti - The Laws of Manu with The Bhasya of Medhatithi.* Calcutta: Calcutta University, 1920)

[48] J. Hastings, *Encyclopaedia of Religion and Ethics.* New York:

Scribner's Sons, 1926, p. 450.

[49] D. D. Dhillon, *Sikhism, Origin and Development*. New Delhi: Atlantic Publishers & Distributors, 1988.

[50] M. al-Munāwi, *Faydh al-Qadīr Sharh al-Jami' Al-Saghīr*, 2nd ed. Beirut: Dar al-Ma'rifah, 1972.

[51] A. Al-Shātibī, *Al-Muwāfaqāt*. Cairo: Dar Ibn al-Qayyim / Dar Ibn 'Affan, 2003, vol 3, p. 79 / vol 2, p. 11.

[52] M. Abu Zahrah. *Al-Fiqh Al-Islāmī*. Cairo: Al-Majlis al-'A'la li-Shu'un al-'Islami, p. 35.

[53] Ibid

[54] S. Thahabi, *Siyar A'lam al-Nubala*. Cairo: Dar al-Hadith, vol 3, p. 428.

[55] B. Al-'Ayni, *'Umdah l'Qari*. Beirut: Dar Ihya al-Turath al-Arabi, vol 16 p. 250.

[56] A. al-Nasāi, *Sunan al-Nasā'ī*. Hadith number 281.

[57] M. al-Bukhāri, *Saḥīḥ al-Bukhāri*, vol 1, Hadith number 297, p. 67.

[58] M. Muslim, *Saḥīḥ Muslim*, Hadith number 746.

[59] Ibn al-Manthur. *Lisān al-'Arab 12/ 497-496*. Dar al-Ma'arif.

[60] Ibid. 12/503

[61] *Lisān al-'Arab*. Pg 3781. Op. Cit.
See also: al-Asfahāni, Abu'l Qasim al-Husain b. Muhammad. *Al-Mufradāt*. Maktabah al-Anjlu al-Misriyyah. Pg 628. Critical editor: Dr Muhammad Ahmad Khalfullah.

[62] *Al-Mu'jam al-Wasit*. Pg 768.

[63] Lisān al-'Arab. 3782. Op.Cit.

[64] Al-Zubaidi, Muhammad b. Muhammad, al-Husaini. *Taj al-'Urus Min Jawahir al-Qamus*. Pg 1/7868.

[65] *Al-Tawqif 'ala muhimmaā al-Ta'arif.* Pg 278.

[66] Al-Fayruzabādi, Majd al-deen Abu Tahir Muhammad b. Ya'qub. *Basā'ir thawi't tamyeez fi lata'if al-kitāb al-'Aziz.* Pg 1/1286. Critical editor: Muhammad 'Ali al-Najjār. Ihya al-Turath al-Islamiyy.

[67] Al-Jassās, 'Ali b. Ahmad Abu Bakr. *Ahkām al-Qur'an.* 3/ 138-139. Critical edit: Muhammad al-Sādiq Qamhawiy. Dar Ihya al-Turāth al-'Arabi. 1405 H.
See also: Al-Tabari, Jarir b. Muhammad. *Jami' al-bayān fi ay ta'wil al-Qur'an.* 8/ 290-291. Critical edit: Ahmad Shakir. Mu'assasah al-Risālah. 1st edition. 2000.
See also: Al-Zamakhshari, Abu-l'Qasim Jar al-Allah Mahmud b 'Umar. *Haqā'iq al-tanzil.* 1/ 523. Dar Ihya al-Turāth al-'Arabi. Critical edit: 'Abdurrazzāq al-Mahdi.

[68] Al-Sa'di, 'Abd Al-Rahman b. Nasir. *Taysir al-Karim al-Rahman fi tafsir kalam al-Mannān.* 101, 177. See also: Ridha, Muhammad Rashid 'Ali. *Tafsir al-Manār.* 5/55-56, 2/302. Al-Hay'ah al-Misriyyah al-'Āmah lil Kitab. 1990.
See also: B. 'Ashur, Muhammad al-Tahir. *Al-Tahrir wa al-Tanwir.* 5/38.

[69] Ibn 'Arabi, Abu Bakr, Muhammad b. 'Abdullah. *Ahkām al-Qur'an*, 2/336. Dar al-Kutub al-'Ilmiyah (Beirut). Muhammad 'Abdul Qadir 'Ata.

[70] Ibn 'Atiyyah, Abu Muhammad 'Abdulhaqq b. Ghālib. *Al-Muharrar Al-Wajiz*. 4/41.

[71] Al-Zamakhshari, al-Kashshāf, 1/ 538. Op. Cit.

[72] Al-Tha'labi, Abu Ishāq Ahmad b. Muhammad. al-Kashf wal Bayan. 3/ 303. Dar Ihya al-Turāth al-'Arabi (Beirut). Critical edit: Muhammad b. 'Ashur. 2002. 1st Edition.

[73] Al-Baghdadi, 'Ala al-deen 'Ali b, Muhammad. Tafsir al-Khazin. 1/519. Dar al-Fikr. 1979.

[74] Al-Qurtubi, Muhammad b. Ahmad. *Al-Jami' l'Ahkām al-Qur'an*. 5/170. Dar 'ālim al-Kutub. Critical edit: Hisham Samir al-Bukhari. 2003.

[75] Al-mahalli, Jalal al-deen Muhammad b. Ahmad & al-Suyuti, Jalal al-deen, 'Abdurrahman b. Abi bakr. *Tafsir al-Jalalain*. 1/105. Dar

al-hadith. 1ˢᵗ edition.

76 Al-Mawardi, Abu'l Hasan 'Ali b. Muhammad. *Al-Nukat wa'l 'Uyun*. Dar al-Kutub al-'Ulumiyyah (Beirut). Critical edit: al-Sayyid b. 'Ali.

77 Musnad Ahmad (5869)

78 Ibn 'Arabi, Abu Bakr, Muhammad b. 'Abdullah. *Ahkām al-Qur'an*, 2/336. Op. Cit. See also: Al-Qurtubi, Muhammad b. Ahmad. *Al-Jami' l'Ahkām al-Qur'an.* 5/170. Op. Cit.

79 Sahih Muslim (143), Abu Dawud (4122), Ibn Majah (4034)

80 Ibn Faris, Abu'l Husain Ahmad. *Mu'jam Maqayis al-Lughah.* Dar al-Fikr. Critical Edit: 'Abdussalam Muhammad Harun. 1979. 4/69.

81 Ibid.

82 Ibn Manthur. Lisan al-'Arab. 11/458. Op. Cit.

83 De Beauvoir, Simone. *The Second Sex*. Vintage Books, London. 2011. Pg 44.

[84] Abu Shuqqah, Abd-l'Halil Muhammad. *Tahrir al-mar'ah fi 'asr al-risalah.* 281/1. Dar al-Qalam. 7th edition. 2011.

[85] Ibn al-Qayyim al-Jawziyyah, Muhammad b. Abi Bakr. *Al-Turuq al-Hukmiyyah fi al-Siyasah al-Shar'iyyah.* Pg. 34. Critical edition: Muhammad Jamil Ghazi.

[86] Ibid.

[87] Henry, Julie D., and Peter G. Rendell. "A review of the impact of pregnancy on memory function." *Journal of Clinical and Experimental Neuropsychology* 29.8 (2007): 793-803.

[88] Al-Razi, Fakhr al-Din Muhammad. 'Umar. *Mafātih al-Ghayb.* 7/89. Dar Ihyā al-Turāth al-'Arabi. 3rd edition. 1420.

[89] Loftus, E.F., Banaji, M.R., Schooler, J.W. and Foster, R., 1987. *Who remembers what?: Gender differences in memory.* Ann Arbor: University of Michigan. *Michigan Quarterly Review, 26, p. 79*

[90] Al-'Iraqi, Abu al-Fadhl 'Abduraheem b. al-Husayn, Al-tabsirah

wa al-Tathkirah, Dar ibn al-Jawzi. Pg 28, 1st edition.

91 Mohammad Akram Nadwi, *al-Muhaddithāt: The Women Scholars in Islam* (Oxford: Interface Publications, 2007).

92 Al-Thahabi. *Mizān al-I'tidal fi naqd al-rijāl.* 5/460.

93 Ibn Hajr, Abu'l Fadhl Ahmad b. 'Ali al-'Asqalani. *Lisan al-Mizān.* 7/522. Hijriyyah Manshurat Mu'assasah al-'Ilmi lil Matbu'at (Beirut). 3rd edition. 1986.

94 Ibn al-Qayyim al-Jawziyyah, Muhammad b. Abi Bakr. *I'lām al-muyaqqi'in 'an Rabb al-'Alamin.* 5/90-103. 1973 (Beirut).

95 Ibn Qudāmah, Muwaffaq al-deen 'Abdullāh b. Ahmad. *Al-Mughni.* 10/162. 1985- Dar Ihyā al-Turāth al-'Arabi. 1st edition.

96 Al-Buhuti, Mansur b. Yunus. *Kashshāf al-Qina' 'An Matn al-'Iqna'.* 9/ 2828. Critical edit: Ibrahim Ahmad al-Sabi'. Dar 'Alam al-Kutub (Riyadh). 2003.

97 al-Shirbini, Muhammad al-Khatib. *Mughni al-Muhtāj.* 3/448.

Dar al-Fikr.

[98] Al-khattab, Muhammad b. Muhammad. *Mawāhib al-Jalil lisharh Mukhtasar al-Khalil.* 5/ 561. Dar 'Alam al-Kutub (Riyadh). 2003.

[99] Ibn al-'Arabi. *Ahkām al-Qur'an.* Op.Cit.

[100] Al-Jassās. *Ahkām al-Qur'an* (3/149). Op .Cit. Also: al-Qurtubi. *Al-Jāmi' l'Ahkām al-Qur'an.* (5/170). Op. Cit. Al-Shawkāni, Muhammad b, 'Ali. *Fath al-Qadir.* 1/531. Dar Ibn Kathir/ Dar al-Kalim al-Tayyib. Damascus. 1414 H. 1st edition. Al-Nasafi, Abu Barakat 'Abdullah b. Ahmad. *Madārik al-Tanzil wa Haqā'iq al-Ta;wil.* 1/314. Al-Maktabah al-Islamiyyah (Beirut).

[101] Al-Tabari. *Tafsir al-Tabari.* 8/ 290. Op-Cit.

[102] Al-Zubaidi. *Taj al-'Urus Min Jawāhir al-Qamus,* 1/5427-5426. Also: *Lisan al-'Arab.* 8/ 240. Op Cit. *al-Qamus al-Muhit* 1/ 962. *Mukhtar al-Sihah* 1/ 927

[103] Abu Hayyān, Muhammad b. Yusuf al-Andalusi. *Al-Bahr al-muhit fi'Tafsir.* 3/686. Dar al-Fikr. Critcial edit: Sidqi Muhammad Jamil. 1420 H.

[104] Al-Nasafi. *Madārik al-Tanzil wa haqā'iq al-ta'wil*. 1/ 314. Op Cit.

[105] *Musnad Ahmad* 19402

[106] *Bukhari* 7257, *Muslim* 1841

[107] M. al-Munāwi, *Faydh al-Qadīr Sharh al-Jami' Al-Saghīr*, 2nd ed. Beirut: Dar al-Ma'rifah, 1972.

[108] A. Al-Shātibī, *Al-Muwāfaqāt*. Cairo: Dar Ibn al-Qayyim / Dar Ibn 'Affan, 2003, vol 3, p. 79 / vol 2, p. 11.

[109] M. Abu Zahrah. *Al-Fiqh Al-Islāmī*. Cairo: Al-Majlis al-'A'la li-Shu'un al-'Islami, p. 35.

[110] Ibid.

[111] Osman, Mohammed Abu Safiyyah, *On Morality: The Union of the Prophet (PBUH) with 'Ai'sha*. Accessed on 20/03/2019. https://www.salam.org.uk/2018/09/27/on-morality-the-union-of-the-

prophet-pbuh-with-aisha/

[112] Al-Tabari. *Tafsir al-Tabari.* 4/ 123. Op-Cit.

[113] *Sunan Abi Dāwud* 2146, *Sunan al-Dārimi* 2122- Chapter: The prohibition of hitting women.

[114] *Sunan Ibn Mājah* 2060

[115] T. Alkiek, D. Mogahed, O. Suleiman, & J. A. C. Brown, "Islamic Perspectives on Domestic Violence," *Yaqeen Institute for Islamic Research.* Accessed on 22/03/2019: https://yaqeeninstitute.org/en/tesneem-alkiek/islam-and-violence-against-women-a-critical-look-at-domestic-violence-and-honor-killings-in-the-muslim-community/

[116] Al-Qāḍī Abū Bakr b. al 'Arabī, Ahkām al Qur'ān: 1/469, pub, Dār al Ma'ārif, Egypt, Taḥqīq (verified)by 'Alī Muḥammad al-Bijāwī.

[117] Ibid.

[118] Ahmad Shafaat, Tafseer of Surah an-Nisa, Ayah 34 Archived

2002-03-27 at the Wayback Machine, Islamic Perspectives. August 10, 2005

[119] Muhammad 'Imārah, *'Ru'iyah Jadīdah li Ma'nā al-Nushūz'* in *Minbar al- Islam,* Cairo: Ministry of Al-Awqaf: The Supreme Council for Islamic Affairs, Issue Shawwal, 1431/Sept., 2010, pp. 91-

[120] *Mawāhib al-Jalil.* 4/15-16,.Op Cit.

[121] Amina Wadud, *Inside the Gender Jihad: Women's Reform in Islam* (Oxford: Oneworld Publications, 2006), p 79

[122] Badran, Margot, 2007. *Feminism beyond East and West; New Gender Talk and Practice in Global Islam.* New Delhi,:Global Media Publications.

[123] Amina Wadud, *Inside the Gender Jihad: Women's Reform in Islam. Pg* 200. Op. Cit.

[124] *The World's Muslims: Religion, Politics & Society.* Pew Research Center, Washington, D.C. 2013. URL: https://www.pewforum.org/2013/04/30/the-worlds-muslims-

religion-politics-society-women-in-society/

[125] Yusuf, Ahmad. *Ahkam al-Zawaj wa'l Furqah*. Cairo. Maktabah al-Zahra. 1984.

[126] Judith Tucker, *Women, Family, and Gender in Islamic Law* (Cambridge: Cambridge University Press, 2008), p. 96.

[127] Ibn Qudāmah, Muwaffaq al-deen 'Abdullah b. Ahmad. *Al-Mughni*. 7/403. 1985- Dar Ihyā al-Turāth al-'Arabi. 1st edition.

[128] Al-Buhuti, Mansur b. Yunus. *Kashshāf al-Qina' 'An Matn al-'Iqna'*. 9/ 2828. Critical edit: Ibrahim Ahmad al-Sabi'. Dar 'Alam al-Kutub (Riyadh). 2003.
See also: al-Shirbini, Muhammad al-Khatib. *Mughni al-Muhtāj*. 3/443. Dar al-Fikr. And:
Al-khattab, Muhammad b. Muhammad. *Mawāhib al-Jalil lisharh Mukhtasar al-Khalil*. 3/ 589. Dar 'Alam al-Kutub (Riyadh). 2003.

[129] Al-Mawsu'ah al-Fiqhiyyah al-Kuwaitiyyah. Wazarat al-Awqaf wa'sh Shu'un al-Islamiyyah- Kuwait. 32/107. 2nd edition.

[130] M. Ibn Sa'd, *Al-Tabaqat al-Kubra*. (Cairo: Maktabat Khānjī,

2001), vol. 10, p. 195. Note: the chain of transmission (*sanad*) has various types of weakness such as the presence of Raytah, who has been declared *majhul* (unknown), as well as the *irsal* (absent link between the narrator and the Prophet (PBUH)) of 'Amrah (see Ibn Hajr, *Taqrib al-Tahthib*, pg 1355 and 1365, Dar al-'Asimah). However, this does not detract from the meaning of the narration, since it is one that is ever-present within the textual evidences from both the Qur'an and the Prophetic tradition.

[131] Vawter, Bruce. "DIVORCE AND THE NEW TESTAMENT." *The Catholic Biblical Quarterly*, vol. 39, no. 4, 1977, pp. 528–542. Accessed on 18/04/2019 from *JSTOR*, www.jstor.org/stable/43714465.

[132] *Al-Mawsu'ah al-Fiqhiyyah al-Kuwaitiyyah*. Wazarat al-Awqaf wash Shu'un al-Islamiyyah- Kuwait. 3/17.

[133] Salah al-deen Sultan. *Mirath almar'ah wa qadhaiyyh al-musawah*. 1999. Nahdha Misr. See also: Shalabi, Muhammad Mustapha. *Ahkam al-mawarith beyna al-fiqh wa'l Qanun*. Maktabah al-Nasr. 1992.

[134] Almaric Rumsey, *Moohummudan Law of Inheritance and right and relations affecting it: Sunni Doctrine*, 3rd ed. (London: W.H. Allen, 1880) as cited in Alshankiti, Asma. A Doctrinal and Law and Economics Justification of the Treatment of Women in Islamic Inheritance Laws. Masters Thesis. 2012. University of Alberta, Edmonton, Canada.

[135] Mary F. Radford, *The Inheritance Rights of Women Under Jewish and Islamic Law*, 23 B.C. Int'l &
Comp. L. Rev. 135 (2000),
http://lawdigitalcommons.bc.edu/iclr/vol23/iss2/2

S.A.L.A.M
SHARING, AFFECTION, LOVE AND MERCY

Printed in Poland
by Amazon Fulfillment
Poland Sp. z o.o., Wrocław